LONDON

SHERRY MARKER

GREAT CITIES

A BLACKBIRCH PRESS™ BOOK

THE ROSEN PUBLISHING GROUP, INC.

Published by Blackbirch Press™ in conjunction with The Rosen Publishing Group, Inc.
29 East 21st Street, New York, NY 10010

©1990 Blackbirch Press™ a division of Blackbirch Graphics, Inc.
First Edition

Printed in Hong Kong
Bound in the United States of America

Editors: Kailyard Associates
Editorial Assistant: Norma L. Ginsberg
Art Director: Cynthia Minichino
Maps: Robert Italiano

OCT 1991

CODMAN SQUARE

Library of Congress Cataloging-in-Publication Data

Marker, Sherry.
  London / Sherry Marker.
  (Great cities)
  Includes bibliographical references and index.
  Summary: Describes the city of London, its history and people.
  1. London (England)—Juvenile literature. [1. London (England)]
I. Title. II. Series.
DA678.M34 1990   90-38239
942.1′2—dc20   CIP
ISBN 0-8239-1210-8   AC

pages 4–5
The changing of the guard at Buckingham Palace is a daily event filled with pomp and precision. The guards' tall bearskin busbies are worn winter and summer.

CONTENTS

LONDON

Grand Union · REGENT'S PARK · EUSTON STATION · ST. PANCRAS STATION · CORAM'S FIELDS · FARRINGTON RD · BISHOPSGATE · MARYLEBONE STATION · MADAME TUSSAUD'S · PLANETARIUM · UNIVERSITY COLLEGE · UNIVERSITY OF LONDON · BROADCASTING HOUSE · BRITISH MUSEUM · OLD STREET · CHARTERHOUSE · SMITHFIELD MARKET · MOORGATE · PADDINGTON STATION · WALLACE COLLECTION · WIGMORE STREET · HOLBORN · GUILDHALL · BAYSWATER RD · OXFORD STREET · MARBLE ARCH · GROSVENOR SQUARE · SOHO SQUARE · ROYAL OPERA HOUSE · LINCOLN'S INN FIELDS · ST. PAUL'S CATHEDRAL · BANK OF ENGLAND · KENSINGTON GARDENS · The Round Pond · The Serpentine · HYDE PARK · PARK LANE · ROYAL ACADEMY · NATIONAL GALLERY · COVENT GARDEN · FLEET STREET · THE MONUMENT · TOWER OF LONDON · KENSINGTON PALACE · ROTTEN ROW · KNIGHTSBRIDGE · PICCADILLY · TRAFALGAR SQUARE · CHARING CROSS STATION · River Thames · London Bridge · BILLINGSGATE MARKET · Tower Bridge · COLLEGE OF SCIENCE AND TECHNOLOGY · ROYAL ALBERT HALL · HYDE PARK CORNER · KENSINGTON RD · GREEN PARK · BUCKINGHAM PALACE · ST. JAMES'S PARK · DOWNING STREET · WATERLOO STATION · BLACKFRIARS RD · WATERLOO RD · BOROUGH HIGH ST · OLD TOWER BRIDGE RD · SCIENCE MUSEUM · NEW SCOTLAND YARD · HOUSES OF PARLIAMENT · N · NATURAL HISTORY MUSEUM · VICTORIA ST · WESTMINSTER ABBEY · LAMBETH RD · OLD KENT RD · CROMWELL RD · FULHAM RD · KING'S RD · VICTORIA STATION · WESTMINSTER CATHEDRAL · TATE GALLERY · LAMBETH PALACE · IMPERIAL WAR MUSEUM · ¼ · ½ · Mi. · ½ · 1 Km.

SCOTLAND · North Sea · UNITED KINGDOM · NORTHERN IRELAND · IS. OF MAN · IRELAND · ENGLAND · NETHERLANDS · WALES · London · BELGIUM · ATLANTIC OCEAN · English Channel · FRANCE

CITY OF LONDON

Emblems such as this coat of arms for London appear everywhere—on soldiers' uniforms, banners, and above the shops of honored merchants.

Population: 6.8 million.

Size: 625 square miles. Largest city in Great Britain.

The City of London: The oldest part of London, covering about one square mile, is in the heart of London. The city of London (known as "the City") is administered by the Corporation of London, made up of a Court of Common Council consisting of the Lord Mayor, 24 aldermen, and 130 common councilmen. The Lord Mayor is elected by Common hall, made up of masters and wardens of livery companies, which are London's ancient craft guilds. The City is the financial heart of London, with the Bank of England, the Stock Exchange, and many insurance companies.

Ethnic Makeup: Inner London has 34.4 percent ethnic minorities and outer London has 29.4 percent. Overall, Greater London has 25.5 percent ethnic minorities, the majority from commonwealth countries and Pakistan. London has sizeable Arabic, Chinese, Greek, and Irish communities as well.

Official City Motto: Each borough and the City has its own motto. The motto of the City is *Domine Dirige Nose* (God Guide Us). The City's emblem is a dragon.

Industry and Commerce: Until World War II, London was the banking, shipping, and insurance capital of the world. Today, London increasingly draws revenue from tourism.

Parks: There are some 20,000 acres of parks including the 5,900 acres of the royal parks in central London such as St. James's Park, Hyde Park, Kensington Gardens, and Regent's Park, as well as Hampstead Heath and Richmond Park on London's peripheries.

Universities: The University of London (with twenty colleges and some 60,000 full-time students), City University, Brunel University, and the London Graduate School of Business Studies.

THE PLACE

An aerial view of London and the River Thames. The Tower Bridge is in the foreground with the Tower of London to its right. The other bridges are, in order, London Bridge, the railway bridge, Southwark Bridge, and Blackfriars Bridge. Waterloo Bridge is around the first bend.

Historians like to say that "geography is destiny." That's certainly true of London, which straddles the River Thames in southeast England, forty miles inland from the North Sea. Across the North Sea from the mouth of the Thames is another great river: the Rhine. Travelers and traders have always sailed down the Rhine River, across the North Sea, and into the Thames. London's location on the Thames destined it to become not only the most important trade center in England, but one of the most important ports in the world.

London grew up at the one spot on the Thames that met two important conditions for trade and commerce: (1) the Thames was deep enough to allow big merchant vessels to anchor, and (2) this was the only place where a bridge could be built across the river. For most of its 230 miles the Thames banks are soft, but where London is built there are gravel beds to support the weight of a bridge. With the Thames bridged, goods could be transported from London throughout the British Isles.

The Thames is London's best-known river, but several other rivers run through the city. These smaller rivers were London's first highways. People and merchandise moved easily throughout London on its rivers. Today, most of these rivers have been channeled to run under London, but their presence is revealed by street names such as Fleet and Walbrook.

Many of London's first buildings were built of wattle and daub, a mixture of twigs and clay. The clay came from the banks of the Thames, and the twigs came from nearby forests. The soil around London is rich in clay but has almost no stone. The nearest quarries are sixty miles away in Kent, and stones had to be brought to London either along the Thames on barges or overland on carts and sledges. The Romans had the technology to do this, but after they left London in the fifth century A.D., stone was not widely used for building until the seventeenth century.

London's forests, with their mighty oak trees, are long gone, although more than 20,000 acres have been set aside as parks. That's almost thirty-two square miles of parks in central London. By contrast, New York City's Central Park is only 1.25 square miles; twenty-four Central Parks would fit into London's parks. The great eighteenth-century statesman William Pitt called these parks "London's lungs."

A wide variety of trees and plants grow in London's parks and gardens. More than 1,835 species of flowering plants and ferns have been counted within twenty miles of St. Paul's Cathedral. All those plants provide nourishment and sanctuary for London's 160 species of birds. London's best-known birds are the pigeons, which flock around Trafalgar Square. Today's pigeons are the descendants of the ones that the

Romans raised for food. The cries of starlings, white-headed gulls, and migratory geese and ducks are commonly heard in the city as well. London is home also to a number of small animals, including hedgehogs, squirrels, and bats. Even foxes have been spotted in London's parks and seen scampering through the tunnels of the underground railway.

Ask Londoners what the climate is like, and they'll probably reply that anyone who spends a day in town will see it all: rain, chill, and drizzle, alternating with what locals call "sunny intervals." London's climate is mild enough (annual temperatures fluctuate between 42° and 65° F) for daffodils to be in bloom throughout the entire city by St. David's Day (1 March). London is wet enough that at least twenty-three inches of rainfall is measured each year in St. James's Park. In fact, Londoners regard more than a few days without rain as near drought conditions.

All in all, London weather is so changeable that it is the main topic of conversation almost every day for almost all Londoners. Here's one example: in 1990, London was having the mildest winter since 1600—until temperatures plummeted, and a freak hurricane hit the city. Many weather recorders speculated that this odd weather was caused by the greenhouse effect, which may be causing worldwide weather changes. Most Londoners, however,

Early spring flowers in St. James's Park.

Bright red, double decker buses squeeze through the city's narrow, congested streets.

The Tower of London has served purposes ranging from a prison for Anne Boleyn to the repository of the Crown Jewels.

thought that the hurricane was just another example of their changeable weather.

The outline of London on a map has been compared to a squashed tomato, spreading out on both sides of the Thames. The center of the "tomato" is where London began as a small settlement on the north bank of the Thames. Gradually the city spread, first west along the north bank and then across the river to the south bank. The land on both sides of the Thames is largely level, although St. Paul's cathedral occupies a slight hill. The terrain rises to its highest point (460 feet) at Highgate in North London.

The heart of London is the square mile known as "the City," on the north bank of the Thames. This is where London's earliest settlements were located. Just outside the City is Westminster, where most government offices are located. Westminster is part of today's central London, which contains most of the city's famous landmarks: St. Paul's, the Tower of London, Buckingham Palace, the Houses of Parliament, and Westminster Abbey. Most of London's parks are to be found in central London, as are the financial, governmental, and most fashionable residential districts.

Today's London is a city made of 33 villages (known as *boroughs*). Most of London lies beyond the City and beyond central London, stretching out into the English countryside for more than 600 square miles on both sides of the Thames. (New York City, by comparison, has only 5 boroughs and covers only 365 square miles.) One reason for London's physical size can be attributed to the maxim "An Englishman's home is his castle." Not surprisingly, most homes are single-family units.

London grew so fast in the early decades of the twentieth century that many people became concerned that it would soon devour the countryside. In 1935, more than 1,200 miles encircling London were set aside as a "Green Belt," which prohibits large-scale building development. Outside the Green Belt, however, more than a dozen new towns have been founded. Every day more than a million commuters travel from outside the Green Belt into central London by car, train, underground (subway), and bus. In addition, old districts of London, such as the docklands, are being transformed into residential districts. City planners hope that future residents will live in new homes along the Thames, where the first settlers lived in prehistoric times.

London's subway system is officially called the underground, but most Londoners call it "the tube." It is the quickest and easiest way to get around the city.

THE PAST

Above all rivers thy river hath renown,
Where many a swan doth swim with wings fair,
Where many a barge doth sail and row with oar,
Where many a ship doth rest with top royal.
O town of townes, patron and not compare,
London, thou art the fairest of cities all.

—William Dunbar (1460–1520)

According to royal custom, London Bridge is lit up to celebrate
a royal marriage.

The first people to live where London is today came from Europe during the Old Stone Age (ca. 250,000 B.C.). These Stone Age people were nomadic hunters and gatherers, who killed wild animals with their flint weapons and gathered grains for food. Around 8000 B.C., much of the North Sea silted up, and Britain was joined to Europe by a marshy plain. With the open sea gone, European settlers crossed the plain easily and settled in the Thames Valley.

Around 6000 B.C., the North Sea cut through the plain, and land traffic between Britain and Europe was cut off. This meant that travel back and forth from England to Europe was only possible by a dangerous sea journey. As a result, the people in the Thames Valley began to live in settlements of simple wattle and daub huts. Soon they were growing food, and keeping animals for meat.

During the Bronze Age (ca. 1300 B.C.), these early settlers learned how to make bronze tools from local mineral deposits. They exported bronze swords, which archaeologists call the "Thames type," throughout Europe. Around 300 B.C., the area began to decline in importance, as iron replaced bronze for use in weapons and tools. There were no iron deposits along the Thames, and by the time that the Romans arrived in Britain, few people lived in the Thames Valley.

This painting of London in the 1400s gives us some idea of what the city looked like at that time.

Roman London

No one knows when London got its name, or what the word means. When the Romans invaded Britain in A.D. 43, they called the spot where they built a bridge across the Thames "Londinium" (London). At first, Roman London was simply an army camp, but gradually, a permanent trading settlement with docks, shops, and houses grew up.

In A.D. 60, London was destroyed when Boudicca, the queen of the native Iceni tribe, led a revolt against the Romans, who had annexed her kingdom. Many Romans fled, but those who did not escape were massacred. Many skulls have been found in the Walbrook, suggesting that Boudicca's troops decapitated their enemies. Two years later, the Romans defeated Boudicca. The queen took poison to avoid being taken as a prisoner.

After Boudicca's defeat, the Romans decided to make London the most important city in Britain. By A.D. 80, London had a new forum (market place) with an enormous basilica (administrative center) flanked by army barracks, houses, shops, temples, baths, and theaters. The Roman historian Tacitus described London in the first century A.D. as busy with "merchants and trading vessels."

In the second century A.D., the Romans built walls to protect London from hostile local tribes. The walls were eight feet thick and twenty feet high, with massive gates and towers. They enclosed a semi-circular area of some 326 acres on the north bank of the Thames. A building tile found with the Latin inscription "Ausalis has been wandering away from work for two weeks" reveals that not all laborers enjoyed their work. It also reveals that common laborers knew enough Latin to scribble insults!

When they weren't working, Roman Londoners seem to have enjoyed relaxing at the circus, just as they did in Rome: a pair of small leather bikini bottoms, probably belonging to a child acrobat, were found in a well in Queen Street. Many Roman Londoners also attended ceremonies honoring the Persian god Mithras. By the third century A.D., London had a large temple to Mithras. The temple was rediscovered and excavated in 1954. Even after

Christianity was introduced to Britain in the fourth century A.D., Londoners continued to worship Mithras.

Most Londoners lived in simple wattle and daub huts. Wealthier Romans built stone houses with elaborate mosaic floors, central heating, and running water. One governor, Agricola, encouraged the native Britons to take up the Roman habit of daily hot baths. Under the Romans, Londoners enjoyed some conveniences and comforts that they would not have again until central heating and indoor plumbing returned in the twentieth century.

By the fourth century, London was the fifth largest city in the western Roman Empire, with a population of more than 50,000. Early in the fifth century, however, the Romans left England as their huge empire began to collapse. During the next century, London was almost entirely deserted. Little is known about this period, but a house that was excavated on Lower Thames Street does tell us something about what London life may have been like after the Romans left. This splendid fourth-century house, with central heating and an elegant bathroom, was a wreck by the late fifth century. Windows broke and were not replaced, and the roof collapsed, and was never repaired. Squatters seem to have lived in the house. Probably the squatters had fled to London from the countryside to escape two invading tribes, the Angles and the Saxons.

Medieval London

The Anglo-Saxon period (from the fifth to eleventh centuries), which followed the Roman occupation, takes its name from the Angles and Saxons. So little is known of London during the fifth to ninth centuries that they are known as the Dark Ages. This is the period of the legendary hero Beowulf and of King Arthur. We don't even know if Arthur was a real king or a legendary figure like Beowulf. We do know that St. Paul's Cathedral was founded in 604 by the missionary bishop Mellitus. In the eighth century, London was important enough that one historian called it "a market for many people coming by land and sea."

Some of those who came by sea were Danish pirates (the Vikings), who repeatedly attacked London over the course of the next four centuries. In 878, King Alfred the Great drove the Danes from London. Over the next two centuries, the Danes attacked and seized London again and again. Finally, King Edward the Confessor drove them out in 1042. Edward made London his capital, and built a splendid new palace at Westminster. Edward also founded Westminster Abbey, but the first king to be crowned there was a foreigner, William the Conqueror.

In 1066, William, the Duke of Normandy, king of what today is France, conquered England and earned the nickname "the Conqueror." To protect London, William ordered "strongholds to be built

against the fickleness of the vast and fierce popu-
lace." One of these, the White Tower, built of white
stone William imported from Caen, France, still
forms part of the Tower of London.

London developed many of the institutions that
shaped its history during the medieval period. In
1191, King Richard's brother, John, who would
become King eight years later, gave London the right
to elect its own mayor. King John probably regretted
this in 1215, when he was forced to sign the
Magna Carta. The Magna Carta stated that the king
had to share his power with the nobles, and it au-
thorized the mayor of London to make sure that the
king obeyed.

Westminster, shown in this seventeenth century etching, is comprised of
the Hall, the two Houses of Parliament, and the Abbey (the church).
Many of England's greatest poets are
buried within the Abbey, and many of
the nation's greatest speeches have
been delivered in Parliament.

Parlament House   the Hall   the Abby

One of London's most important medieval institutions was the guilds, which were part trade schools and part social clubs. These guilds trained apprentices, looked after members who fell on hard times, and elected the Lord Mayor of London. Every conceivable trade—from fishmonger, tailor, tanner, and baker to goldsmith and diamond cutter—had its own guild. By 1400, there were 110 guilds in London. The guilds were so important that London's town hall (built 1411-1440) is still called the Guildhall.

One guild member who made a name for himself—and became one of the City's most famous mayors—was Dick Whittington. As the story goes, Whittington was an orphan, with only a pet cat to keep him company. Young Whittington almost left London when he couldn't find a job. As he climbed Highgate Hill on his way out of town, Whittington thought he heard the bells of St.-Mary-le-Bow Church call out "Turn Back, Dick Whittington, Thrice Lord Mayor of London." Whittington returned to London and made his fortune. It's a good story, but in fact, Whittington was neither an orphan nor poor, although he did make a great fortune and was elected Lord Mayor of London three times between 1397 and 1420.

In medieval London, each profession occupied a different quarter, which meant that each guild was in a different neighborhood. Wealthy guilds competed with each other to build the most elegant churches. By the end of the twelfth century, London had more than 126 guild churches and was called "the city of steeples."

During the medieval period, new roads were built from London across all England. In 1209, a modern stone structure was completed to replace the old wooden bridge across the Thames. This bridge, known as "Old London Bridge," stood until 1832 and was London's *only* bridge until 1750. With new roads and a new bridge, London again became one of the most important cities in Europe.

By the fourteenth century, London was fast becoming a city of villages. The old Roman walls were tumbling down and hamlets were encircling the City.

During the 1500s, Britain was a strong sea power and London one of the world's busiest seaports.

The bubonic plague, or Black Death, struck Europe in 1348, killing fifty thousand people in London alone.

Despite these new settlements, the City itself remained overcrowded, and most streets were open sewers. At least two-thirds of London's population died during a plague carried by rats, known as the Black Death, in 1348–9. Fifty thousand Londoners were buried in mass graves outside the City.

One Londoner who escaped the plague was England's first great poet, Geoffrey Chaucer (1342–1400). Chaucer's *Canterbury Tales* describes the adventures of pilgrims traveling from London to the great cathedral at Canterbury. Chaucer worked at London's Customs House and wrote in his spare time. Recently, a house from Chaucer's period was excavated next to the Customs House. The house is known as the Merchant's House, after the wealthy merchant Chaucer describes in *The Canterbury Tales*. The house had its own chapel, a counting house, warehouses, and a central courtyard, in addition to a kitchen and several bedrooms and sitting rooms. Unlike the Roman house on Lower Thames Street, however, the medieval house did not have central heating.

Still, in medieval London, it was possible for someone born to humble origins, like Dick Whittington or Geoffrey Chaucer, to win fame and fortune. Not even the plague could stop London's growth. As Daniel Defoe, the author of *Robinson Crusoe*, wrote, "How much further may London spread? Who knows!"

Geoffrey Chaucer was born in London around 1340. He is considered the greatest poet of the Middle Ages and is best known for his masterpiece, *The Canterbury Tales*, a group of stories in verse that satirized the medieval church.

Tudor London

From 1485 until the death of Queen Elizabeth I in 1603, England was ruled by the Tudor dynasty. In 1533, Elizabeth's father, Henry VIII, broke with the Catholic Church and seized fifty rich monasteries and abbeys in London, keeping much of what he took for himself. The Archbishop of York's London palace beside the Thames, which Henry confiscated in 1529, became his Palace of Whitehall. Whitehall covered twenty-three acres and was as large as a small village. The palace was so enormous that visiting dukes were given nine beds for their servants and stables for twenty-four horses. With Henry living at Whitehall, the old palace of Westminster built by Edward the Confessor was empty. Parliament, the English legislative body, made Westminster its meeting place.

Henry also gave a good deal of land to his supporters. Many built themselves fine palaces near the palace of Whitehall; others sold portions of their land. As a result, there was an explosion of building. By the end of Henry's reign, London's population had grown from perhaps 40,000 to 90,000. By the end of Elizabeth's reign, more than 75,000 people lived inside London's old walls, with another 150,000 in the new villages outside the walls.

At least one Londoner, John Stow, didn't like the way the city was growing. Stow wrote in his *Survey of London* (1598) that too much of London was being

King Henry VIII broke away from the Catholic Church in 1533 because the Pope would not allow him to divorce his wife Catherine of Aragon and marry Anne Boleyn.

covered with "filthy cottages" and "alleys of small tenements," which attracted "beggars and other loose persons." By 1600, London had thirty-seven almshouses for beggars and almost as many orphanages for abandoned children. Hospitals had charity wards, which were often too crowded to take new patients. Conditions at St. Mary's Bethlehem Hospital for the insane were so bad that the hospital's nickname, "Bedlam," came to be synonymous with the worst sort of madhouse.

Despite widespread poverty, London enjoyed a golden age under Elizabeth I. Elizabeth's courtiers included Sir Francis Drake, who sailed around the world, and Sir Walter Raleigh, who defeated the

Queen Elizabeth I, the daughter of Henry VIII and Anne Boleyn, reigned during what is commonly regarded as England's golden age, 1558–1603.

Spanish Armada, colonized Virginia, searched for the legendary land of El Dorado, wrote a *History of the World*—and was executed in the Tower of London in 1618 for treason by her successor, James I. Elizabeth's contemporaries included the poet John Donne, who served as Dean of St. Paul's Cathedral, and the playwright William Shakespeare, whose plays were first performed in the Globe Theater in Southwark, in South London.

Stuart London and Civil War

From 1603–1714, England was ruled almost exclusively by monarchs of the House of Stuart. This was an exciting period in London. In 1605, Guy Fawkes tried to blow up the Houses of Parliament in protest of laws against Catholics. In 1642, civil war broke out and Oliver Cromwell led a successful revolt against King Charles I. Charles had a brilliant court—he hired the painter Van Dyck and the architect Inigo Jones to beautify his London residences—but he ignored, and even dissolved, Parliament when it refused to do his bidding. Many suspected Charles of wanting to be an absolute monarch.

One hundred thousand Londoners turned out to cheer in 1649 when Charles was condemned to death as a "Traitor, Tyrant and Public Enemy." When the king was beheaded on the threshold of his palace at Whitehall, no one in the huge crowd protested. As a contemporary political pamphlet stated, "If posterity shall ask who could have pulled the crown from the King's head, taken the government off its hinges, dissolved the monarchy, enslaved the laws and ruined the country—say 'twas the proud unthankful rebellious city, of London."

After Cromwell's death in 1658, the monarchy was restored, ending England's brief experience as a republic. A few years later, two events occurred that almost brought an end to London itself: the Great Plague of 1665 and the Great Fire of 1666. Up to

William Shakespeare (1564-1616) is usually considered the greatest dramatist of the English language. He came to London sometime between the years of 1585 and 1592 to begin his career in the theater.

Oliver Cromwell, who ruled the British Commonwealth from 1649–1658, was one of the first European leaders to establish religious toleration.

100,000 Londoners died in the plague (10,000 in the week of August 31 alone), and more than four-fifths of the city was destroyed in the fire.

The fire began in a baker's shop in Pudding Lane and raged through London's narrow streets, crowded with half-timber buildings with overhanging upper stories. Flames leapt easily from building to building and raced down narrow lanes. Almost 400 acres burnt to the ground, destroying more than 13,000 houses and eighty-seven churches, including St. Paul's Cathedral. The debris was still smoldering six months later, hampering clean-up work and preventing rebuilding. Tens of thousands of refugees spent a miserable winter in tents hastily erected in the outlying London villages.

Not since Queen Boudicca burnt London in A.D. 60 had the city been so badly damaged. London writer Samuel Pepys (1633–1703) described both the plague and the fire in his diary. Pepys pointed out that the "horrid, malicious, blood flames" had one immediate beneficial result: it put an end to the plague. While the city was still smoldering, Londoners realized that the disastrous fire gave them the opportunity to rebuild the city so that it would be better than ever—and safe from future fires.

The Rebuilding Act of 1667 stated that no house could exceed four stories, and it outlawed wooden houses and overhanging upper stories. London was to be built of stone and brick, with timber used only for woodwork. King Charles II announced a contest to design the new city, and prominent architects submitted plans. None of the plans was adopted, and London was never rebuilt with the wide boulevards and straight streets Charles favored.

The person who had the greatest influence on the new London was a young architect named Christopher Wren. Wren won contracts to rebuild fifty-one churches, including St. Paul's Cathedral. It took thirty-five years to rebuild St. Paul's, and most Londoners hated the new cathedral because its massive dome reminded them of St. Peter's in Rome. Protestant Londoners didn't want their cathedral to look anything like a Catholic church. Nevertheless, St. Paul's dome eventually became the symbol of London, just as the Eiffel Tower is the symbol of Paris.

By 1700, the population of London was 680,000. Trading companies, like the East India Company and the Royal Africa Company, brought goods from all over the world into London's new markets at Covent Garden and the Royal Exchange. You could buy anything from a glass eye to a fur cape at the markets, which teemed with shoppers, tourists, prostitutes, and pickpockets. Around the markets were London's new coffee houses, which served as social clubs and informal business offices. The Bank of England handled much of the world's finances, and London's insurance companies insured most of the world's ships.

Christopher Wren, the architect of St. Paul's Cathedral, was severely criticized for the church's "Catholic look."

Despite the loss of the American colonies, England's overseas trade tripled between 1720 and 1820.

In short, many modern institutions were in place by the time George I came to the throne in 1714. The penny post was introduced in 1681, and London got its first daily newspaper, the *Daily Courant*, in 1702. By the end of the century, London had a number of daily newspapers. A German visitor to London remarked that "the English would, I think, go without breakfast or supper rather than neglect their morning or evening papers."

During the seventeenth century, London homes began to get piped water. The service only operated three days a week, but even this made a great difference to London's sanitation. People could wash clothes and dishes more easily—and even take baths! Ironically, piped water may have contributed to the last great fire of the century, which destroyed the Royal Palace at Whitehall in 1698. The palace burnt to the ground when a chambermaid set fire to some clothing she had just washed and was drying by a fire. Only the banqueting hall, designed by Inigo Jones, was saved. Work began almost immediately on new royal palaces, which were built in London's Kensington and St. James's districts.

Eighteenth Century London: The Hanoverian Dynasty

When George I came to the throne in 1714, the population of London was 490,000. By the end of the century, there were almost one million Londoners. London expanded beyond the City and Westminster into what was called the West End. City planners laid out large, open squares. One of the first, Hanover Square, was named in honor of the new king, who was a member of the house of Hanover. Hanover Square, Grosvenor Square, and Bedford Square were enclosed by uniformly planned rows of houses. Trafalgar Square was a center of commerce and a meeting place for many London roads.

Three brothers—John, James, and Robert Adams, heavily influenced by the great architect Inigo Jones's use of classical motifs—designed many eighteenth-century buildings in what came to be called the Georgian style. One handsome Georgian house was built by Robert Walpole, the first Earl of Oxford and a member of Parliament—with, his enemies revealed, stolen funds. In 1703, the Duke of Buckingham built an elegant townhouse called Buckingham House. In the nineteenth century, the English monarchy took over Buckingham House, enlarged it, and renamed it Buckingham Palace.

Most Londoners, of course, continued to live simply. Dr. Johnson wrote his great dictionary of the English language in such a modest house on Gough Square. The brick four-story house, built in 1700, conformed to the rebuilding code of 1667. The wood used for the doors and beams was white and yellow pine, brought back as ballast from the American colonies in ships that had sailed there filled with English goods.

Along with London's growth in size and population came an enormous growth in trade and industry. Many of London's best-known banks, businesses, schools, and hospitals were founded during the eighteenth century. Trade through the port of London tripled between 1720 and 1820, although the

Buckingham Palace has been the home of England's monarchy since 1837. During the tourist season, the palace is surrounded by people eager to catch a glimpse of Queen Elizabeth II.

American Revolution interrupted trade with those colonies. Within a few years, merchants who had dealt with America were trading instead with Canada, India, and the West Indies. At the same time, trading became more diversified as shipping-related industries—rope, hemp, and sail making—began to produce for other markets. Navigational instruments,

The British Museum, housing everything from ancient Greek ruins to rare postage stamps, is one of the world's finest museums.

clocks, and watches made in London were prized throughout the world. In fact, the Swiss watch industry got started producing cheap imitations of the valuable London watches.

While the American and French revolutions were going on abroad, London was in the midst of a scientific revolution. London became a world center for studies and inventions in the fields of navigation, botany, and medicine. The Royal Botanical Gardens at Kew were founded in 1761, and English explorers like Captain Cook brought back samples from around the world. In 1759, another great institution of learning opened its doors: the British Museum, founded with the gift of physician Hans Sloane's enormous personal library. By 1800, there were more than 2,000 circulating libraries in London.

Despite advances in science and learning, poverty was never far beneath the surface in eighteenth-century London. Newgate Prison, opened in 1670, was expanded several times to accommodate the legions of prostitutes, pickpockets, and debtors who lived there. Many did not stay long: arson, forgery, and harming cattle were among the crimes that carried the death penalty.

Nineteenth Century London: The London of Queen Victoria

No monarch was to rule as long as Queen Victoria, who came to the throne as a girl of eighteen in 1837 and died at the age of eighty-two in 1901. During Victoria's reign, England's empire stretched around the world. As capital of the British Empire, London was the most important city in the world. Londoners boasted that "the sun never sets on the British Empire." Queen Victoria was a symbol of changelessness and continuity during a century when London changed almost unimaginably. During Victoria's reign, London's population rose from just under one million to 4.5 million, and the city grew to cover almost 130 square miles (London today covers 600 square miles).

During the Victorian era, four enormous new docks were constructed along the Thames, and by 1869, London had more shipyards and engine makers than any other city in the world. For the first time, London had metropolitan fire and police brigades. The scientific and cultural advances of the eighteenth century continued, with the opening of the National Gallery, University College, the Natural History Museum, and concert halls like the Royal Albert Hall. The Elementary Education Act of 1870 mandated that all children attend school until age ten, although many did not.

Two new forms of transportation emerged during the Industrial Revolution, which transformed London during the nineteenth century: the railroad in the 1830s and the underground in the 1860s. As the novelist Thackeray wrote, "Your railroad starts a new era . . . . We who lived before railways and survive out of that ancient world are like Father Noah and his family out of the Ark."

Trains took over much of the work of canal barges and ships to speed goods throughout Britain. In 1863, the underground railway opened its first line, between the City and Paddington. On the first day, 30,000 Londoners travelled to work by underground, greatly relieving the congestion in London's streets. The next year, the underground sold 12 million tickets. Today the underground is one of the best subway systems in the world.

Inventions like this Nasmyth steam hammer propelled England toward the rapid changes of the Industrial Revolution.

The Royal Albert Hall, with its giant rotunda 700 feet in circumference, is a popular spot for concerts of all kinds.

In the nineteenth century, crowding and unsanitary conditions in London's slums made life wretched for the city's poor.

The railway and underground also meant that Londoners could live further away from work. The construction of both the railway and underground lines destroyed thousands of London homes. Many middle-class Londoners moved out to the new suburbs, while the poor crowded into existing neighborhoods. Social reformers like Octavia Hill (1838–1912) worked to persuade Parliament to improve these inner-city neighborhoods. Dame Henrietta Barrett encouraged the building of "garden suburbs" with affordable housing for the poor. Unfortunately, such efforts were infrequent.

London's poverty influenced two famous immigrants, Karl Marx and Frederich Engels, to found the Communist League in 1847–8. Native Londoner Henry Mayhew wrote a grim account of what life was like for most Londoners in *London Labour and the London Poor* (1861). Children worked twelve-hour days in match factories, or roamed the streets collecting old rags or selling vegetables and fruit. Many were alcoholics, and spent part of their earnings in London's "gin houses." Some worked as "mudlarks," sifting through the muddy banks of the Thames for scrap metal. One mudlark Mayhew interviewed was a homeless six-year-old orphan.

Most orphans led desperate lives. Only a few made their way to charitable institutions like Dr. Barnabo's home for Destitute and Neglected Boys, founded in 1871. Poor girls hoped to work in the homes of the wealthy. By 1851, one-third of all London women were employed in domestic service. They worked long hours and earned little, but they were more fortunate than those who turned to prostitution to support themselves.

Charles Dickens also gave a grim picture of life in London's poor neighborhood in novels like *Oliver Twist* (1839). Young Oliver spent his early years in a poorhouse, where he was always hungry. When Oliver once asked for a second serving of watery porridge, he was severely punished. Dickens understood Oliver's situation all too well: Dickens himself had worked as a child laborer in a boot-blacking factory when his father was sent to debtors' prison.

By the time that he wrote *Oliver Twist*, Dickens's novels had brought him fame, and he was living in middle-class comfort in a house with running water on Doughty Street. Dickens and his family were fortunate. Most Londoners got their water in buckets from the Thames or from public pumps that were turned on only a few minutes a day.

London's weak water system allowed another terrible fire to burn out of control, and in 1834 the Palace of Westminster burnt to the ground. It took twenty-eight years (1840–1868) to rebuild the Houses of Parliament. When they were done, London had another famous landmark: the clock tower nicknamed Big Ben after Sir Benjamin Hall, then London's Commissioner of Works.

The Old Curiosity Shop was immortalized in Charles Dickens' 1841 novel of the same name.

London's water supply was also filthy. One hundred miles of sewers pumped raw sewage directly into the Thames. As recently as 1858, known at the time as "the year of the great stink," Parliament, the English legislative body, had to adjourn because of the overpowering stench from the Thames.

Londoners also complained that their drinking water tasted bad and smelled bad. In fact, residents thought that the water's smell (or *miasma*, as they called it) caused cholera. In 1850, Dr. John Snow proved that the cholera epidemic, then causing 400 deaths a day, was caused not by smelling but by drinking polluted water. Despite Dr. Snow's discovery, it took another twenty-eight years before London's water supply was treated.

In 1851, London celebrated the Great Exhibition of the Works of Industry of All Nations in the enormous new Crystal Palace, built under the supervision of Queen Victoria's husband, Prince Albert. More than 6 million people came to London to see the more than 17,000 exhibits. The Crystal Palace took its name from the more than 400 tons of glass used in its roof and windows. The technology to build such an enormous building using so much glass had been unknown only a few years earlier. After the Great Exhibition, the Crystal Palace, with its zoos, theaters, concert halls, exhibitions, and restaurants, was one of London's most popular amusements until its destruction by fire in 1936.

Twentieth Century London

For much of the twentieth century, England enjoyed a second Elizabethan Age, under Queen Elizabeth II. The young queen came to the throne in 1952. Another London exhibition, the Festival of Britain, celebrated both Elizabeth's coronation and London's recovery from World War II. By the 1980s, some of Queen Elizabeth's subjects were speculating that she might reign as long as queen Victoria, an idea not popular with everyone. Some felt that the Queen should abdicate in favor of her son Prince Charles.

As London's population climbed to over 6.7 million, the Prince spoke openly of the need to protect London from the excesses of growth and the destruction of the environment. His outspoken statements led some to dismiss him as a crank, while others praised him as the "green" prince, for his commitment to environmental issues.

Almost every aspect of life in London changed radically during the twentieth century. The "modern" gas lights and coal fires of the Victorian era were replaced by electric lights and gas-fired central heating. With coal no longer used for heating, London lost its famous pea-soup fogs, which had been caused by pollution from coal smoke.

At the beginning of the twentieth century, most Londoners got their news from daily papers; by the 1940s, almost every home had a radio, and by the 1980s, almost every home had at least one television.

Sir Winston Churchill flashes the "V-for-victory" sign during World War II.

Many magazines, popular from the 1930s to the 1960s, disappeared in the eighties, as Londoners read less and watched the "telly" more. Many movie theaters, which Londoners had flocked to in the 1950s, closed, as people stayed home. The music halls and pantomime theaters, so popular in the nineteenth century, also closed, or were revived only at holidays like Christmas.

World War I (1914–18) and World War II (1939–45) changed London enormously. England had fought in many overseas wars, but now the war came home to London. German bombs fell on London during World War I, killing 2,000, injuring several thousand, and destroying many buildings in the City. This was nothing compared to what happened in World War II during the bombing known as the Blitz. Twelve thousand tons of bombs fell on London between August of 1940 and March of 1945. Almost 30,000 Londoners were killed, twice that many were injured, and 12,000 buildings were destroyed. In all, almost three-fifths of the City was destroyed during the Blitz—almost as much as in the Great Fire of 1666.

The face of London changed almost beyond recognition during post-war rebuilding in the 1950s and 1960s. In the City, especially in the East End docklands area, which had been heavily bombed, twenty-story skyscrapers were built. Entire neighborhoods, which were formerly marked by winding streets

Between 1940 and 1945, German planes bombed London, destroying most of the city. This was known as the Blitz.

lined with houses with small gardens, were replaced by impersonal high-rise housing estates. Many of these were subsidized public housing, known as council houses.

The new council houses often had modern conveniences that the old homes lacked, but almost no one wanted to live in them. An Englishman's home was still his castle, and people compared the multi-family

47

Prince Charles and Lady Diana on their wedding day. The British monarchy preserves English tradition through custom and ceremony.

dwellings to "rabbit hutches." Those who could afford it moved to new homes in the suburbs. By the 1980s, much of London's post-war housing had become a desolate urban slum. Things got so bad that many apartments were torn down and replaced with smaller homes, which Londoners found more congenial.

Nonetheless, for much of the century, Londoners seemed to believe that bigger was better. Large department stores, like Woolworths and Marks and Spencers, sold a wide variety of goods under one roof. Supermarkets like Sainsburys replaced the corner butcher, green grocer, and baker. In the 1970s, American-style shopping malls were built outside London itself. The shopping malls reflected the fact that Londoners increasingly traveled by private car. In 1934, cars were so rare that the only traffic light in all London was on Kensington High Street. By 1990, environmentalists like Lord Tordoff were predicting that the level of carbon dioxide in London's air would double by the year 2001 and "choke London to death."

Despite, or perhaps because of, the enormous changes in London during the twentieth century, nostalgia for the past increased as the eighties drew to a close. With the loss of the British Empire, London was no longer the most important city in the world. Air transport and container shipping suddenly made London's great docks old-fashioned. London lost its place as the center of world finances as first New York and then Tokyo became more important. Tourism—an industry built in large part on nostalgia for the past—became increasingly important for London.

During the twentieth century, many social ills were improved. Londoners had clean water, extensive public transportation, subsidized public housing, a new national health system, and free education for children to age sixteen. Yet Prince Charles was not the only one who felt that London was in danger of destroying its past and endangering its future. As the new millenium approaches, Londoners are concentrating on environmental and social issues in the hope of keeping London the "fairest of cities all."

THE PEOPLE

O London is a dainty place,
A great and gallant city!
For all the streets are paved with gold,
And all the folks are witty.
                    —**Street Ballad, 1789**

Although the English monarchy retains no political power, popular support for the Queen is strong. As a result, she can often sway public opinion on issues of national importance.

One of England's greatest nineteenth-century prime ministers, Benjamin Disraeli, said that "London is a nation, not a city." Just as the United States has always been a country of immigrants, London is a city of immigrants. Like the United States, London has always been a "melting pot" for many different nationalities. But the "melting" process isn't always smooth. Often old-comers regard newcomers with suspicion.

Roman Londoners regarded the Angles and Saxons as barbarians, and the Angles and Saxons were suspicious of the French who came over with William the Conqueror. In the late Middle Ages, Italian merchants from the district of Lombardy and Jewish traders and bankers from Spain met hostility. In fact, the Jews were exiled from London in 1290 and allowed to return only in the seventeenth century. During the nineteenth century, hundreds of thousands of Jews fled to England to escape persecution in Europe. Most settled in London, where their different language, religion, and customs seemed odd to many Londoners. In 1906, Parliament passed a bill limiting Jewish immigration to 4,000 a year.

The Jewish refugees were not the first to be unpopular in London. In the eighteenth century, more than 7,000 American colonists loyal to the King emigrated to London. Samuel Quincy, the Solicitor General of Massachusetts, fled to London and boasted that he saw "many faces I have been used to.

America seems to be transported to London." While the presence of so many other Americans made Quincy feel at home, Londoners were less pleased with what they saw. Merchant Edward Oxnard complained that St. James's Park was "thronged with refugees."

One thing that the English didn't like about the Americans was that they clung to their own customs, even importing favorite foods from America. A Mrs. Hutchinson of Massachusetts wrote home that she and her fellow refugees "continued to live as much in the New England way as we can." These American refugees, of course, spoke English—although an old joke says that "America and England are two countries divided by a common language." During World War II there were many American G.I.'s in London. The British government distributed pamphlets urging Londoners not to "make fun of the Americans' accents or vocabularies."

The problems for non-English-speaking immigrants to London are even more complicated. From the Middle Ages until the nineteenth century, immigrants from Europe often lived in ghettos, where they had little need to learn English. In the late nineteenth century, laws were passed that all children had to go to school until they were ten. Non-English-speaking children had to "sink or swim" in London schools. Today, most schools offer help for children whose first language is not English. In

Big Ben, a London landmark, watches over the activity of the city.

some inner-city schools, more than forty languages can be heard.

After World War II, there was a great need for cheap labor to help rebuild London. Workers were recruited from commonwealth countries in the West Indies, Guyana, India, Pakistan, and Bangladesh. Most of these workers were non-white. By 1971, as had happened earlier in the century, many Londoners became worried by this large influx of foreigners. Parliament passed an immigration act that virtually halted commonwealth immigration.

London's long history of immigration is best symbolized by one house in the City, on Princelet Street. In 1718, Londoner Samuel Worrall built a house here for Peter Ogier, a Huguenot (Protestant) refugee from Catholic France. Ogier was a prosperous silk weaver, who planted mulberry trees in his courtyard so that he could raise his own silk worms. In 1862, Ogier's family had made enough money to move out of the City. The house was bought by new immigrants, a family of Polish Jews. This family built a small synagogue in the courtyard, and stayed until the 1950s. Since then, the house on Princelet Street has been owned by Bengali immigrants, who built a small mosque nearby. Today, the house on Princelet Street is a Heritage Center for the study of London's changing population.

London's markets have also reflected its varied heritage. Since the Middle Ages, Londoners have

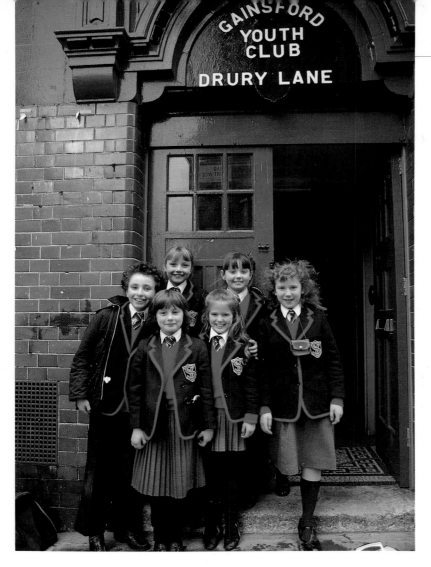

London schoolchildren such as these grow up with their city's history surrounding them; some buildings date back to the eleventh century.

been able to buy German food in one neighborhood, Italian in another, and Spanish in yet another. Today, Brixton in south London has Caribbean street markets. Petticoat Lane in the City and Portobello

Guards at the Tower of London, called Yeoman Warders, are commonly known as "Beefeaters."

Road off Notting Hill Gate both have street markets where you can buy anything from apples to antiques. In Chinatown, there are restaurants where the menus are only in Chinese, and around Earl's Court, only Arabic is spoken in many shops.

London's major food markets were located in the City until the 1970s, when most were moved to the outskirts to cut down on traffic into central London. Only a few remain in central London, including the meat market at Smithfield and a general provisions market at Leadenhall. Here and there throughout the City there are mobile markets: vendors selling jellied eels, fruits, vegetables, and flowers from push-carts. Many vendors are cockneys, Londoners born within the sound of the bells of St. Mary-le-Bow in Cheapside. Cockneys have a distinctive accent and often use a rhyming slang when they don't want to be understood. London vendors have been known as *costermongers* (from the costard apple) since the Victorian era. Some stalls have been in the same family for generations, although street vendors and musicians are increasingly a thing of the past in London.

The great English historian Thomas Carlyle wrote, "The history of the world is but the biography of great men." Certainly, London has had more than its share of great men and women. Still, the history of London is not just the history of queens like Boudicca, the two Elizabeths, and Victoria. Nor is it the history of famous politicians like Disraeli and Churchill, writers like Dickens and Dr. Johnson. London is a mosaic made up of all its people.

Often, all that we know of ordinary Londoners who lived prior to the twentieth century is their names and dates of birth and death as recorded on tombstones. But the information explosion that has taken place during this century has given us detailed information on almost every facet of life. Newspapers, photographs, and movies, as well as army, medical, job, and school records provide us with a rich look at the lives of ordinary Londoners. Here's one example: Schoolboy Stanley Ludder's essay on being fitted for a gas mask on 6 October 1939 is preserved in the Museum of London. From the essay, we learn that Stanley was one of many children evacuated from the East End to the country to escape the Blitz.

Stanley Ludder was born a Londoner, but most of today's Londoners are born elsewhere, some in towns and villages across Britain, others in the commonwealth nations. Two such Londoners are Norwell Roberts, London's first West Indian policeman, and Margaret Thatcher, England's first woman Prime Minister. Norwell Roberts was born on the little West Indian island of Anguilla, and Margaret Thatcher was born in Grantham, in Lincolnshire, in the English Midlands. Yet, like so many before them—including Dick Whittington—each chose to become a Londoner.

ON THE TOUR BUS

Landmarks

There's no one thing that symbolizes London, as the Eiffel Tower does Paris, or the White House does Washington, D.C. Instead, a number of places mean London. *St. Paul's Cathedral*, *Buckingham Palace*, and *Big Ben* are probably the most famous landmarks—but don't forget the *Tower of London*, *Nelson's Column* in *Trafalgar Square*, and even the *River Thames* itself.

St. Paul's Cathedral, top of Ludgate Hills. For centuries, the cathedral dominated London from its slightly elevated site in the City. In recent years, skyscrapers have threatened to obscure St. Paul's massive dome.

Tower of London, on Tower Hill. Where some of London's most famous prisoners were kept—and where the Crown Jewels are on display today.

Big Ben, the *Houses of Parliament*, and *Westminster Abbey* cluster just outside the City in Westminster. Here you will find some of London's most famous landmarks, each with a rich history. Westminster Abbey is perhaps the most potent symbol of English monarchy, serving as the place where most English sovereigns have been crowned and buried.

A stroll along *Whitehall*, a half-mile thoroughfare that separates Westminster from Charing Cross, takes you past the scene of King Charles's execution and into *Trafalgar Square*. From there, you can easily visit *St. James's Palace* and *Buckingham Palace*, the latter being the residence of the Queen.

A statue of Winston Churchill, Prime Minister of England during World War II, stands in Parliament Square.

Parks

Green Park and *St. James's Park*. Perhaps because they are so near St. James and Buckingham palaces, these two rank as London's most elegant parks, with beautifully maintained gardens and ponds filled with ducks, geese, pelicans, and black and white swans. Feeding time is the ideal time to see the water-fowl.

Hyde Park, at the west end of Piccadilly. Covering an area of 361 acres, the park is a favorite of Londoners, who frequent the Serpentine, an artificial lake where swimming and boating are allowed; Speakers' Corner, where orators hold forth; and Rotten Row, a sand-track for horseback riders.

Kensington Gardens, bordering Hyde Park. This was Peter Pan's favorite park, or at least the favorite park of his creator, J. M. Barrie. There is a statue of Peter Pan in the park, which is the traditional spot for Kensington nannies to promenade the babies in enormous carriages.

A boat trip up and down the River Thames is a favorite pastime for Londoners and visitors alike.

Museums

Museum of London, London Wall, at the Barbican. Exhibits range from Roman coins and wooden water pipes to taxis and The Lord Mayor's Stage Coach. If you want to follow the course of the old Roman wall, begin here—parts of the wall touch the museum itself. Excellent walking tours of London leave from the Museum most weekends.

British Museum, Great Russell Street, Bloomsbury. London's best-known museum has no equal in the world for the diversity and quality of its contents. It seems to have at least one of everything, including mummies, manuscripts, and marble statues.

Natural History Museum, Cromwell Road, South Kensington. Comprised of five departments, each with its own library and student room—botany, entomology, zoology, mineralogy, and palaeontology.

Science Museum, Exhibition Road, South Kensington. A wide-ranging collection—from machinery to scientific instruments to hot-air balloons—that includes a Children's Gallery. A favorite for school field trips.

Geological Museum, Exhibition Road, London. First established in Whitehall in 1851, the museum now houses a magnificent display of gemstones, plus models of some of the world's most famous stones. There is also an audiovisual display that shows the origins of the earth.

Victoria and Albert Museum, Cromwell Road, London. A superb collection of medieval art and furniture and costumes of all periods.

National Gallery, Trafalgar Square, London. One of the great galleries in the world, containing European paintings from all schools and every period.

National Portrait Gallery, St. Martin's Place, London. Paintings and photographs of Britain's monarchs, heroes, and scoundrels.

Royal Academy of Arts, in the Burlington House, just off Piccadilly. Exhibits contemporary painting, sculpture, architecture, and engraving.

Two new museums reflect London's position as a world capital of entertainment. The *Theater Museum*, Covent Garden, has stage settings, photos of famous actors, and theater memorabilia. In the South Bank complex, the *Museum of the Moving Image* is a lively museum chronicling the history of cinema.

You might think that's more than enough museums for one city, but London has lots more! There's the *Museum of Mankind*,

A traditional English breakfast often includes kippers, salmon, sausage, ham, and eggs.

6 Burlington Gardens, with exhibits of tribal and village cultures; the *Imperial War Museum*, on Lambeth Road, with airplanes and tanks; the *London Transport Museum*, in Covent Garden, with buses and trams; the *Tate Gallery*, on Millbank, devoted to British art; and the *Commonwealth Institute*, on Kensington High Street, devoted to exhibits provided by each Commonwealth government. The *Bethnal Green Museum of Childhood*, on Cambridge Heath Road, has a fine collection of doll houses, more than 4,000 dolls, and teddy bears of all sizes and shapes.

Most of London's museums are public, but two of the best known are private: *Madame Tussaud's*, on Marylebone Road, and the *London Dungeon* at 34 Tooley Street, S.E. 1. Madame Tussaud's has realistic waxwork figures of famous Londoners, like Jack the Ripper and Margaret Thatcher, as well as international political leaders and pop stars. If Madame Tussaud's doesn't satisfy your curiosity about Jack the Ripper, visit the London Dungeon, which specializes in the re-creation of London's ghoulish and gory past.

Famous Shops

Almost everyone wants to visit *Harrods* in Knightsbridge, the world's largest department store. Harrods boasts that it can arrange anything from a christening to a funeral at short notice. For years, the food department delivered a soft-boiled egg each morning to a customer who didn't want to be bothered cooking his own egg! Harrods toy department is quite stupendous, but just across town on Regent Street is *Hamley's*, the world's largest toy store. This is where to go if you want to buy a child-sized, electric-powered Rolls Royce.

The world-famous Harrods department store offers a wide range of luxury food and goods.

Events

Changing of the Guard, Buckingham Palace. Daily in summer, alternate days in winter.

Ceremony of the Keys. Performed nightly, this is the official locking of the Tower of London. On foggy nights, it's easy to imagine how prisoners' hearts must have sunk at the sound of the enormous keys locking them in for another night.

Execution of King Charles I. On the Sunday nearest to January 29, King Charles's execution is celebrated with a parade held by the King's Army, a society that reenacts civil war battles. The procession follows the king's last walk from St. James's Palace to the Banqueting Hall at Whitehall, before moving into Trafalgar Square to lay a wreath at the foot on Charles's statue.

Pearly Harvest Festival. The Pearly Kings and Queens were— and still are—street vendors who ornament their clothes with countless buttons made of mother-of-pearl. October.

Lord Mayor's Show. A parade through the City celebrating the inauguration of the new Lord Mayor. November.

Guy Fawkes Night. November 5 is the anniversary of Guy Fawkes's attempt to blow up the Houses of Parliament.

250,000 B.C.	First Stone Age emigrants from Europe to the Thames Valley.	1192	Election of the first Lord Mayor of London.
A.D. 43	Roman Emperor Claudius invades Britain; London founded; the Thames is bridged.	1209	Completion of Old London Bridge.
		1269	Completion of Westminster Abbey.
60	Queen Boudicca destroys London, which the Romans rebuild.	1305	Establishment of Parliament in its modern form.
		1348	Plague kills 50,000 Londoners.
400	Romans begin leaving Britain; Angles and Saxons invade London.	1399–1461	House of Lancaster.
		1461–1485	House of York.
450–1066	Anglo-Saxon London.	1485–1603	House of Tudor.
604	Founding of St. Paul's Cathedral.	1509–1547	Reign of Henry VIII, who breaks with the Catholic Church and seizes the property of London's monasteries and abbeys; Palace at Whitehall established.
878	King Alfred the Great defeats the Danes.		
1042–66	Reign of King Edward the Confessor, who makes London his capital.		
		1558–1603	Reign of Queen Elizabeth I: Golden age in London after defeat of Spanish Armada. Shakespeare's first plays performed at the Globe Theater.
1066–1154	Norman Period.		
1066	William the Conqueror crowned King of England at Westminster Cathedral.		
1132	London receives a royal charter giving it a Lord Mayor and rights of self-government.	1603–1714	House of Stuart.
		1605	Guy Fawkes's plot to blow up Houses of Parliament fails.
1154–1399	The Plantagenet Dynasty.	1649	Execution of Charles I at Palace of Whitehall.
1156	London officially declared the capital of England.		

1665	The Great Plague.	1910–	House of Windsor.
1666	The Great Fire.	1915–18	World War I; 2,000 die in bombing of London.
1714–1901	House of Hanover.		
1820–28	London gets four new docks and becomes busiest port in the world.	1939–45	World War II; 30,000 die in bombing of London (the Blitz).
		1952	Queen Elizabeth II comes to throne.
1836	London gets its first trains and train station.	1965	Greater London Council replaces the London County Council of 1888–9.
1837–1901	Reign of Queen Victoria: British Empire at its height, and London the most powerful city in the world.		
		1968	London paralyzed by strikes.
		1986	Greater London Council dissolved; London administered by borough councils and Corporation of the City of London.
1851	The Great Exhibition of the Works of Industry of All Nations.		
1888–9	Creation of London County Council to administer Greater London; the City retains its independence and Mayor.	1987	Freak hurricane severely damages London; Kew Gardens loses many ancient trees.
1901–10	House of Saxe-Coburg.	1990	Severe storm again severely damages London.
1904	Meeting in London of World Federation for Women's Suffrage.		

For Further Reading

Briggs, Asa. *They Saw It Happen, Volume IV 1897–1940*. Blackwell, 1960.

Charles-Edwards, T. and Richardson, B. *They Saw It Happen, Volume III 1689–1897*. Blackwell, 1965.

Glanville, Philippa. *Tudor London*. Museum of London, 1979.

Hanson, Michael. *2000 Years of London*. Country Life Limited, 1967.

Hassall, W. O. *They Saw It Happen, Volume I 55 B.C.–1485*. Blackwell, 1955.

Hibbert, Christopher. *London: The Biography of a City*. Allen Lane, 1972.

Kent, William. *An Encyclopedia of London*. Dutton, 1937.

Merrifield, Ralph. *A Handbook to Roman London*. Museum of London, 1978.

Mitchell, R. J., and Leys, M. D. R. *A History of London Life*. Penguin, 1963.

Pritchett, V.S. *London Perceived*. Harcourt, Brace, and World, 1962.

Routh, C. R. N. *They Saw It Happen, Volume II 1485-1688*. Blackwell, 1956.

Trease, C. *London: A Concise History*. Thames and Hudson, 1975.

Heren, L. *Growing up Poor in London*. Hamish Hamilton, 1973.

Hughes, M. V. *A London Child in the 1870s*. Oxford. *A London Girl in the 1880s*. Oxford. *A London Home in the 1890s*. Oxford.

Mayhew, H. *Selections from London Labour and the London Poor*. Oxford, 1965.

Where to Get More Information

British Tourist Authority in the United States:
Chicago
BTA
John Hancock Center, Suite 3320
875 North Michigan Avenue
Chicago, Illinois 60611

Dallas
BTA
Cedar Maple Plaza, Suite 210
2305 Cedar Springs Road
Dallas, Texas 75201-1814

New York
BTA
40 West 57th Street
New York, New York 10019

Useful organizations in London:

City of London Information Center, St. Paul's
    Churchyard, London ECAM 8BX
Guildhall Library, Aldermanbury, London EC2P 2EJ
Museum of London Education Office, 150 Wall,
    London EC 2Y 5HN
The Slide Center, 143 Chatham Road, London SW11
    6SR

INDEX

Photo credits
Cover, p. 14, 33, Steve Vidler/Leo de Wys Inc.; p. 3 (top), 8-9, 41, 56,
courtesy of the British Information Services; p. 3 (middle), 16-17, the
Ashmolean Museum, Oxford; p. 3 (bottom), 50-51, R. Nolan/Leo de
Wys Inc.; p. 4-5, 43, Arthur Hustwit/Leo de Wys Inc.; p. 6, John Lamb/
Leo de Wys Inc.; p. 12, 15, Bob Krist/Leo de Wys Inc.; p. 13, 53,
Fridman Damm/Leo de Wys Inc.; p. 19, 23, 25, 34, 37, New York Public
Library; p. 26, the Bettmann Archive; p. 27, 42, Private Collection; p. 29,
Lady Ashcombe, Sudley Castle, Winchcombe, Gloucestershire,
England; p. 30, the Marquess of Salisbury; p. 31, from the RCS Collec-
tion, with the permission of the Governors of the Royal Shakespeare
Theatre; p. 32, the British Library; p. 38, 59 (bottom), courtesy of the
British Tourist Authority; p. 40, Science Museum Library, London; p. 46,
47, Imperial War Museum, London; p. 48, A. Reininger/Leo de Wys
Inc.; p. 55, 59 (top), Everett Johnson/Leo de Wys Inc.; p. 58, Van
Phillips/Leo de Wys Inc.; p. 60, Karen McCunnall/Leo de Wys Inc.

Photo Research: Photosearch, Inc.